I'm A Little

Written by T. Childers
Illustrated by Iram Adnan

This book is dedicated to Kari, Austin, and Hunter. Who is always there for me. Also, to my Katy Bug, for whom this little song was made for when swimming on the boat all those summers.

My name is Stan the otter, and I don't like the water. I have always been smaller than the other otters my age, and all the other otter kids make fun of me because I can't swim.

It's not that I can't swim, I just never learned how. I am afraid of what I can't see under the water.

I got close once, but some of the otters said they saw an alligator in the water. So I just stood on the bank and watched them swim.

The other otters make fun of me a lot. I am small, and I can't swim. The only friend I have is Ann, and she's a duck. All the other ducks and otters make fun of us for being friends. Ann just tells me not to pay any attention to them.

One day it started raining really hard. It rained for days and days. Everything was wet, and the creek turned into a river. All the ducks and otters were told to stay away from the creek; it was too dangerous.

.

Ann and I were bored after being stuck inside for so many days. We decided to go take a look at the river. We walked through the woods to get a closer look at the top of a cliff. The water was running really fast after all the rain.

Suddenly the cliff we were standing on just broke off. I landed on a rock by the edge of the water, but Ann was swept away downstream by the rushing water.

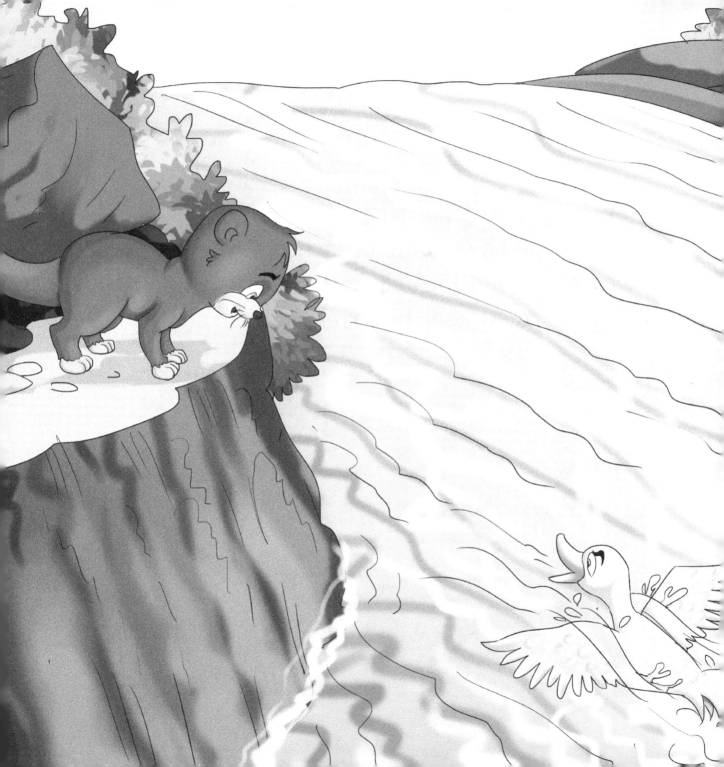

Ann got stuck in some branches in the water. She was screaming for help as loud as she could, but nobody could hear her over the river's loud roar.

.

I climbed up the bank and ran down to the river as fast as I could, but she was too far away from the bank for me to reach her. I tried to climb on top of the branches, but the limbs were too small. I didn't know what to do.

She was being pushed under the water. I had to act before it was too late. I walked in the water as far as I could, and then the most amazing thing happened. I started floating right to the top. It was amazing; I could swim!

I swam around the branches and grabbed Ann. I got her free, and we swam back to shore. She looked at me and said, "You're a little otter swimming in the water." My family and Ann's family were all so happy that I learned to swim that day.

A few days later, the river was a creek again. All the ducks and otters were playing in the water. We ran down the hill and jumped in. We swam and swam all day long.

As we were swimming, we sang our song.
"I'm a little otter swimming in the water, rolling in the waves, you see, won't you come and swim with me?" Soon all the otters and ducks were singing our song with us.

The End.

I'm A Little Otter

CPSIA information can be obtained
at www.ICGtesting.com
Printed in the USA
BVHW020201120123
656158BV00006B/156